Essential Air Fryer Recipes

Most Wanted, Easy and Mouthwatering Recipes for a Healthier Lifestyle

Linda Wang

© **Copyright 2021 by Linda Wang - All rights reserved.**

The content contained within this book may not be reproduced, duplicated or transmitted without direct written permission from the author or the publisher.
Under no circumstances will any blame or legal responsibility be held against the publisher, or author, for any damages, reparation, or monetary loss due to the information contained within this book. Either directly or indirectly.

Legal Notice:
This book is copyright protected. This book is only for personal use. You cannot amend, distribute, sell, use, quote or paraphrase any part, or the content within this book, without the consent of the author or publisher.

Disclaimer Notice:
Please note the information contained within this document is for educational and entertainment purposes only. All effort has been executed to present accurate, up to date, and reliable, complete information. No warranties of any kind are declared or implied. Readers acknowledge that the author is not engaging in the rendering of legal, financial, medical or professional advice. The content within this book has been derived from various sources. Please consult a licensed professional before attempting any techniques outlined in this book.
By reading this document, the reader agrees that under no circumstances is the author responsible for any losses, direct or indirect, which are incurred as a result of the use of information contained within this document, including, but not limited to, — errors, omissions, or inaccuracies.

TABLE OF CONTENTS

INTRODUCTION 1

Scrambled Eggs 5

Tuna and Spring Onions Salad 7

French toast Sticks 9

Treviso Chicory Sauce 11

Pancakes 13

Creamy Mushroom Pie 15

Pear Oatmeal 17

Fish Tacos Breakfast 19

Cheeseburger Sliders 21

Fried Veggies with Golden Polenta Bites 23

Creamy Fennel 25

Roasted Potatoes, Asparagus and Cheese 27

Amazing Peppery Vegetable Omelet with Cheese 28

Cajun Shrimp 30

Breaded Shrimp with Lemon 32

Rice Flour Coated Shrimp 34

Bacon Wrapped Scallops 36

Fish Sticks 38

Spicy Avocado Cod 40

Easy Trout 42

- Beer Coated Duck Breast 44
- Rosemary Chicken Breasts 46
- Chicken Pasta Salad 48
- Flourless Chicken Cordon Bleu 50
- Pork and Sprouts 52
- Beef, Arugula and Leeks 54
- BBQ Pork Ribs 55
- Bacon Wrapped Pork tenderloin 57
- Nut Crusted Rack of Lamb 59
- Crispy Potatoes and Parsley 61
- Sweet and Spicy Parsnips 63
- Sautéed Spinach 65
- Kale and Olives 67
- Sweet & Spicy Parsnips 68
- Air fryer Golden Lentil and Spinach Soup 70
- Japanese Udon Noodle Soup 72
- Air fryer Italian Beef Stew 74
- Crispy Kale Chips (Vegan) 76
- Spicy Chicken with Lemon and Parsley in A Packet 78
- Fennel Spread 80
- Beans and Veggie Burgers 82
- Apple Hand Pies 84
- Brownie Muffins 86

Doughnuts Pudding 88

Chocolate Banana Pastries 90

Apple Tart 91

Crispy Banana Split 93

Delicious Grilled Pineapple 95

Lemon Blueberry Muffin 97

Pecan Brownies 99

NOTES 101

INTRODUCTION

An Air Fryer is a magic revolutionized kitchen appliance that helps you fry with less or even no oil at all. This kind of product applies Rapid Air technology, which offers a new way to fry with less oil. This new invention cooks food through the circulation of superheated air and generates 80% low-fat food. Although the food is fried with less oil, you don't need to worry as the food processed by the Air Fryer still has the same taste like the food fried using the deep-frying method.

This technology uses a superheated element, which radiates heat close to the food and an exhaust fan in its lid to circulate airflow. An Air Fryer ensures that the food processed is cooked completely. The exhaust fan located at the top of the cooking chamber helps the food get the same heating temperature in every part quickly, resulting in a cooked food of better and healthier quality. Besides, cooking with an Air Fryer is also suitable for those individuals which are too busy or do not have enough time. For example, an Air Fryer only needs half a spoonful of oil and takes 10 minutes to serve a medium bowl of crispy French fries.

In addition to serving healthier food, an Air Fryer also provides some other benefits to you. Since an Air Fryer helps you fry using less oil or without oil for some kind of food, it automatically reduces the fat and cholesterol content in food. Indeed, no one will refuse to enjoy fried food without worrying about the greasy and fat content. Having fried food with no guilt is one of the pleasures of life. Besides having low fat and cholesterol, you save some amount of money by consuming oil sparingly, which can be used for other needs. An Air Fryer also can reheat your food. Sometimes, when you have fried leftover and you reheat it, it will usually serve reheated greasy food with some addition of unhealthy reuse oil. Undoubtedly, the saturated fat in the fried food gets worse because of this process. An Air Fryer helps you reheat your food without being afraid of extra oils that the food may absorb. Fried bananas, fish and chips, nuggets, or even fried chicken can be reheated to become as warm and crispy as they were before by using an Air Fryer.

Some people may think that spending some amount of money to buy a fryer is wasteful. I dare to say that they are wrong because an Air Fryer is not only used to fry. It is a sophisticated multi-function appliance since it also helps you to roast chicken, make steak, grill fish, and even bake a cake. With a built-in air filter, an Air Fryer filters the air and saves your kitchen from smoke and grease.

An air Fryer is really a new innovative method of cooking. Grab it fast and welcome to a clean and healthy kitchen.

Scrambled Eggs

Preparation Time: 20 minutes

Servings: 2

Ingredients:

- 4 large eggs.
- 2 tbsp. unsalted butter; melted.
- ½ cup shredded sharp Cheddar cheese.

Directions:

1. Crack eggs into 2-cup round baking dish and whisk. Place dish into the air fryer basket.
2. Adjust the temperature to 400 Degrees F and set the timer for 10 minutes
3. After 5 minutes, stir the eggs and add the butter and cheese. Let cook 3 more minutes and stir again
4. Allow eggs to finish cooking an additional 2 minutes or remove if they are to your desired liking. Use a fork to fluff. Serve warm.

Nutrition:

Calories: 359; Protein: 19.5g; Fiber: 0.0g; Fat: 27.6g; Carbs: 1.1g

Tuna and Spring Onions Salad

Preparation Time: 20 minutes

Servings: 4

Ingredients:

- 14 oz. canned tuna, drained and flaked
- 1 cup arugula
- 2 spring onions; chopped.
- 1 tbsp. olive oil

- A pinch of salt and black pepper

Directions:

1. In a bowl, all the ingredients except the oil and the arugula and whisk.
2. Preheat the Air Fryer over 360 °F, add the oil and grease it. Pour the tuna mix, stir well and cook for 15 minutes
3. In a salad bowl, combine the arugula with the tuna mix, toss and serve.

Nutrition:

Calories: 212; Fat: 8g; Fiber: 3g; Carbs: 5g; Protein: 8g

French toast Sticks

Preparation Time: 10 minutes

Cooking Time: 5 minutes

Servings: 4

Ingredients:

- 4 bread, sliced into sticks
- 2 eggs, gently beaten
- 2 tablespoons soft butter or margarine
- 1 pinch cinnamon
- 1 pinch nutmeg
- 1 pinch ground cloves
- Salt, to taste

Directions:

1. Preheat the Air fryer at 365 °F and grease an Air fryer pan with butter.
2. Whisk eggs with salt, cinnamon, nutmeg and ground cloves in a bowl.

3. Dip the bread sticks in the egg mixture and place in the pan.
4. Cook for about 5 minutes, flipping in between and remove from the Air fryer.
5. Dish out and serve warm.

Nutrition:

Calories: 186, Fat: 11.7g, Carbs: 6.8g, Sugar: 1.7g, Protein: 13.2g, Sodium: 498mg

Treviso Chicory Sauce

Preparation time: 10-20 minutes,

Cooking time: 15-30 minutes;

Serve: 6

Ingredients:

- 400g of Treviso chicory
- ½ red wine
- 1 leek
- Salt to taste

Direction:

1. Chop the leek and place it in the basket previously greased.
2. Cook for 3 minutes at 160 °C.
3. Add the previously cleaned chicory cut into large pieces, pour the red wine and salt. Cook for an added 12 minutes. Ideal for filling pancakes, lasagna, savory cakes, etc.

Nutrition:

Calories 20, Fat 0g, Carbohydrates 4g, Protein 1g

Pancakes

Preparation Time: 30 minutes

Servings: 4

Ingredients:

- 1 cup apple; peeled, cored and chopped.
- 1¾ cups white flour
- 1 egg; whisked
- 1¼ cups milk

- 2 tbsp. sugar
- 2 tsp. baking powder
- 1/4 tsp. vanilla extract
- 2 tsp. cinnamon powder
- Cooking spray

Directions:

1. In a bowl, mix all ingredients: except cooking spray and stir until you obtain a smooth batter
2. Grease your air fryer's pan with the cooking spray and pour in 1/4 of the batter; spread it into the pan.
3. Cover and cook at 360 °F for 5 minutes, flipping it halfway
4. Repeat steps 2 and 3 with 1/4 of the batter 3 more times and then serve the pancakes right away.

Creamy Mushroom Pie

Preparation Time: 20 minutes

Servings: 4

Ingredients:

- 3 eggs
- 6 white mushrooms; chopped.
- 1 red onion; chopped.
- 9-inch pie dough
- 1/4 cup cheddar cheese; grated

- 1 tbsp. olive oil
- 1/2 cup heavy cream
- 2 tbsp. bacon; cooked and crumbled
- 1/2 tsp. thyme; dried
- Salt and black pepper to taste

Directions:

1. Roll the dough on a working surface, then press it on the bottom of a pie pan that fits your air fryer and grease with the oil
2. In a bowl, mix all other ingredients except the cheese, stir well and pour mixture into the pie pan
3. Sprinkle the cheese on top, put the pan in the air fryer and cook at 400 °F for 10 minutes. Slice and serve.

Pear Oatmeal

Preparation Time: 17 minutes

Servings: 4

Ingredients:

- 2 cups pear; peeled and chopped.
- 1 cup milk
- 1/4 cups brown sugar
- 1/2 cup walnuts; chopped.
- 1 cup old fashioned oats
- 1/2 tsp. cinnamon powder
- 1 tbsp. butter; softened

Directions:

1. In a heat-proof bowl that fits your air fryer, mix all ingredients and stir well. Place in your fryer and cook at 360 °F for 12 minutes. Divide into bowls and serve

Fish Tacos Breakfast

Preparation Time: 23 Minutes

Servings: 4

Ingredients:

- 4 big tortillas
- A handful mixed romaine lettuce; spinach and radicchio
- 1 yellow onion; chopped
- 1 cup corn
- 1 red bell pepper; chopped
- 1/2 cup salsa
- 4 white fish fillets; skinless and boneless
- 4 tbsp. parmesan; grated

Directions:

1. Put fish fillets in your air fryer and cook at 350 °F, for 6 minutes
2. Meanwhile; heat up a pan over medium-high heat, add bell pepper, onion and corn; stir and cook for 1 - 2 minutes

3. Arrange tortillas on a working surface, divide fish fillets, spread salsa over them; divide mixed veggies and mixed greens and spread parmesan on each at the end.
4. Roll your tacos; place them in the preheated air fryer and cook at 350 °F, for 6 minutes more. Divide fish tacos on plates and serve for breakfast

Cheeseburger Sliders

Preparation Time: 20 minutes

Servings: 3

Ingredients:

- 1-pound ground beef
- 6 dinner rolls
- 6 slices cheddar cheese
- salt to taste

- black pepper

Directions:

1. Preheat the Air Fryer to 390 – degrees Fahrenheit. Form the ground beef into 6 2.5-ounce patties and season with salt and pepper.
2. Add the burgers to the cooking basket and cook for 10 minutes. Remove from the Air Fryer and place the cheese on top of the burgers and return to the Air Fryer to cook for one more minute.

Fried Veggies with Golden Polenta Bites

Preparation Time: 50 minutes

Servings: 6

Ingredients:

- 1 cup onions; chopped
- 2 cloves garlic; finely minced
- 1/2-pound zucchini; cut into bite-sized chunks
- 1/2-pound potatoes; peeled and cut into bite-sized chunks
- 1/4 cup Cheddar cheese; shaved
- 1 teaspoon paprika
- 1 tablespoon olive oil
- 1/2 teaspoon salt
- 1/2 teaspoon freshly ground black pepper; or more to taste
- 1/2 teaspoon dried dill weed; or more to taste
- 14 ounces pre-cooked polenta tube; cut into slices

Directions:

1. Add the vegetables to an Air Fryer cooking basket.
2. Sprinkle them with olive oil, paprika, salt, pepper, and dill.
3. Now set the machine to cook at 400 - degrees Fahrenheit. Cook for 6 minutes.
4. After that pause the machine, shake the basket and set the timer for 6 minutes more. Set aside.
5. Next spritz the polenta slices with non-stick cooking oil. Spritz the cooking basket too.
6. Set your Air Fryer to cook at 400 - degrees Fahrenheit Air-fry for 20 to 25 minutes.
7. Turn the polenta slices over and cook for another 10 minutes.
8. Top each polenta slice with air-fried vegetables and shaved cheese.

Creamy Fennel

Preparation Time: 17 minutes

Servings: 4

Ingredients:

- 2 big fennel bulbs; sliced
- 2 tbsp. butter; melted
- ½ cup coconut cream
- Salt and black pepper to taste.

Directions:

1. In a pan that fits the air fryer, combine all the ingredients, toss, introduce in the machine and cook at 370 °F for 12 minutes
2. Divide between plates and serve as a side dish.

Nutrition:

Calories: 151; Fat: 3g; Fiber: 2g; Carbs: 4g; Protein: 6g

Roasted Potatoes, Asparagus and Cheese

Preparation Time: 55 minutes

Servings: 2

Ingredients:

- 4 potatoes [medium]
- 1 asparagus bunch
- 1/3 cup crème fraiche [low fat]
- 1/3 cup cheese [cottage]
- 1 tablespoon mustard [wholegrain]

Directions:

1. Add oil and preheat Air Fryer to 390 - degrees Fahrenheit.
2. Cook potatoes in it for 20 minutes.
3. Boil asparagus in salted water for about 3 minutes.
4. Spoon out potatoes and make mash them with rest of ingredients mentioned above.
5. Refill the skins and season with salt and pepper. Serve with rice and enjoy!

Amazing Peppery Vegetable Omelet with Cheese

Preparation Time: 15 minutes

Servings: 2

Ingredients:

- 4 eggs; whisked
- 3 tablespoons plain milk
- 1 teaspoon melted butter

- Kosher salt and freshly ground black pepper; to taste
- 1 red bell pepper; deveined and chopped
- 1 green bell pepper; deveined and chopped
- 1 white onion; finely chopped
- 1/2 cup baby spinach leaves; roughly chopped
- 1/2 cup Halloumi cheese; shaved

Directions:

1. Start with spreading the canola cooking spray onto the Air Fryer baking pan.
2. Add all of the above ingredients to the baking pan, give them a good stir. Then; set your machine to cook at 350 degrees F; cook your omelet for 13 minutes.
3. Serve warm and enjoy!

Cajun Shrimp

Preparation Time: 10 minutes

Cooking Time: 8 minutes

Serve: 4

Ingredients:

- 1 lb shrimp, peeled and deveined
- 1/2 tbsp chipotle chili in adobo, minced
- 1 lime, cut into wedges

- 1 tbsp Cajun seasoning
- 2 tbsp olive oil
- Pepper
- Salt

Directions:

1. Add all ingredients into the large bowl and toss well to coat. Place in the fridge for 1 hour.
2. Spray air fryer basket with cooking spray.
3. Add marinated shrimp into the air fryer basket and cook at 400 °F for 8 minutes.
4. Serve and enjoy.

Nutrition:

Calories 201, Fat 9.1 g, Carbohydrates 3.6 g, Sugar 0.3 g, Protein 26.1 g, Cho10sterol 239 mg

Breaded Shrimp with Lemon

Preparation Time: 15 minutes

Cooking Time: 14 minutes

Servings: 3

Ingredients:

- ½ cup plain flour
- 2 egg whites
- 1 pound large shrimp, peeled and deveined
- 1 cup breadcrumbs
- ¼ teaspoon lemon zest
- ¼ teaspoon cayenne pepper
- ¼ teaspoon red pepper flakes, crushed
- 2 tablespoons vegetable oil
- Salt and ground black pepper, as required

Directions:

1. Preheat the Air fryer to 400 degrees F and grease an Air fryer basket.

2. Mix flour, salt, and black pepper in a shallow bowl.
3. Whisk the egg whites in a second bowl and mix the breadcrumbs, lime zest and spices in a third bowl.
4. Coat each shrimp with the flour, dip into egg whites and finally, dredge in the breadcrumbs.
5. Drizzle the shrimp evenly with olive oil and arrange half of the coated shrimps into the Air fryer basket.
6. Cook for about 7 minutes and dish out the coated shrimps onto serving plates.
7. Repeat with the remaining mixture and serve hot.

Nutrition:

Calories: 432, Fat: 11.3g, Carbohydrates: 44.8g, Sugar: 2.5g, Protein: 37.7g, Sodium: 526mg

Rice Flour Coated Shrimp

Preparation Time: 20 minutes

Cooking Time: 20 minutes

Servings: 3

Ingredients:

- 3 tablespoons rice flour
- 1 pound shrimp, peeled and deveined
- 2 tablespoons olive oil

- 1 teaspoon powdered sugar
- Salt and black pepper, as required

Directions:

1. Preheat the Air fryer to 325 °F and grease an Air fryer basket.
2. Mix rice flour, olive oil, sugar, salt, and black pepper in a bowl.
3. Stir in the shrimp and transfer half of the shrimp to the Air fryer basket.
4. Cook for about 10 minutes, flipping once in between.
5. Dish out the mixture onto serving plates and repeat with the remaining mixture.

Nutrition:

Calories: 299, Fat: 12g, Carbohydrates: 11.1g, Sugar: 0.8g, Protein: 35g, Sodium: 419mg

Bacon Wrapped Scallops

Preparation Time: 15 minutes

Cooking Time: 12 minutes

Servings: 4

Ingredients:

- 5 center-cut bacon slices, cut each in 4 pieces
- 20 sea scallops, cleaned and patted very dry
- 1 teaspoon lemon pepper seasoning
- ½ teaspoon paprika
- Olive oil cooking spray
- Salt and ground black pepper, to taste

Directions:

1. Preheat the Air fryer to 400 degrees F and grease an Air fryer basket.
2. Wrap each scallop with a piece of bacon and secure each with a toothpick.
3. Season the scallops evenly with lemon pepper seasoning and paprika.

4. Arrange half of the scallops into the Air fryer basket and spray with cooking spray.
5. Season with salt and black pepper and cook for about 6 minutes.
6. Repeat with the remaining half and serve warm.

Nutrition:

Calories: 330, Fat: 16.3g, Carbohydrates: 4.5g, Sugar: 0g, Protein: 38.7g, Sodium: 1118mg

Fish Sticks

Preparation Time: 25 minutes

Servings: 4

Ingredients:

- 1 large egg.
- 1 lb. cod fillet; cut into 3/4-inch strips
- 1 oz. pork rinds, finely ground
- ¼ cup blanched finely ground almond flour.
- 1 tbsp. coconut oil
- ½ tsp. Old Bay seasoning

Directions:

1. Place ground pork rinds, almond flour, Old Bay seasoning and coconut oil into a large bowl and mix together. Take a medium bowl, whisk egg
2. Dip each fish stick into the egg and then gently press into the flour mixture, coating as fully and evenly as possible. Place fish sticks into the air fryer basket

3. Adjust the temperature to 400 Degrees F and set the timer for 10 minutes or until golden. Serve immediately.

Nutrition:

Calories: 205; Protein: 24.4g; Fiber: 0.8g; Fat: 10.7g; Carbs: 1.6g

Spicy Avocado Cod

Preparation Time: 20 minutes

- Servings: 2

-

Ingredients:

- 2: 3-oz.cod fillets
- 1 medium avocado; peeled, pitted and sliced
- ¼ cup chopped pickled jalapeños.
- ½ medium lime
- 1 cup shredded cabbage
- ¼ cup full-fat sour cream.
- 2 tbsp. full-fat mayonnaise
- ½ tsp. paprika
- ¼ tsp. garlic powder.
- 1 tsp. chili powder
- 1 tsp. cumin

Directions:

1. Take a large bowl, place cabbage, sour cream, mayonnaise and jalapeños. Mix until fully coated. Let sit for 20 minutes in the refrigerator

2. Sprinkle cod fillets with chili powder, cumin, paprika and garlic powder. Place each fillet into the air fryer basket. Adjust the temperature to 370 Degrees F and set the timer for 10 minutes.
3. Flip the fillets halfway through the cooking time. When fully cooked, fish should have an internal temperature of at least 145 Degrees F
4. To serve, divide slaw mixture into two serving bowls, break cod fillets into pieces and spread over the bowls and top with avocado. Squeeze lime juice over each bowl. Serve immediately.

Nutrition:

Calories: 342; Protein: 16.1g; Fiber: 6.4g; Fat: 25.2g; Carbs: 11.7g

Easy Trout

Preparation Time: 25 minutes

Servings: 4

Ingredients:

- 4 whole trout
- 1 egg; whisked
- 3 oz. breadcrumbs

- 1 tbsp. chives; chopped.
- 1 tbsp. olive oil
- 1 tbsp. butter
- Juice of 1 lemon
- Salt and black pepper to taste

Directions:

1. In a bowl, combine the breadcrumbs, lemon juice, salt, pepper, egg and chives; stir very well.
2. Coat the trout with the breadcrumb mix
3. Heat up your air fryer with the oil and the butter at 370 °F; add the trout and cook for 10 minutes on each side. Divide between plates and serve with a side salad

Beer Coated Duck Breast

Preparation Time: 15 minutes

Cooking Time: 20 minutes

Servings: 2

Ingredients:

- 1 tablespoon fresh thyme, chopped
- 6 cherry tomatoes
- 1 cup beer
- 1: 10½-ouncesduck breast
- 1 tablespoon olive oil
- 1 teaspoon mustard
- 1 tablespoon balsamic vinegar
- Salt and ground black pepper, as required

Directions:

1. Preheat the Air fryer to 390 degrees F and grease an Air fryer basket.
2. Mix the olive oil, mustard, thyme, beer, salt, and black pepper in a bowl.

3. Coat the duck breasts generously with marinade and refrigerate, covered for about 4 hours.
4. Cover the duck breasts and arrange them into the Air fryer basket.
5. Cook for about 15 minutes and remove the foil from the breast.
6. Set the Air fryer to 355 degrees F and place the duck breast and tomatoes into the Air Fryer basket.
7. Cook for about 5 minutes and dish out the duck breasts and cherry tomatoes.
8. Drizzle with vinegar and serve immediately.

Nutrition:

Calories: 332, Fat: 13.7g, Carbohydrates: 9.2g, Sugar: 2.5g, Protein: 34.6g, Sodium: 88mg

Rosemary Chicken Breasts

Preparation Time: 35 minutes

Servings: 4

Ingredients:

- 2 chicken breasts; skinless, boneless and halved
- 1 cup chicken stock
- 1 yellow onion; sliced
- 4 garlic cloves; chopped.

- 2 tbsp. cornstarch mixed with 2½ tbsp. water
- 1 tbsp. soy sauce
- 2 tbsp. butter; melted
- 1 tsp. rosemary; dried
- 1 tbsp. fresh rosemary; chopped.
- Salt and black pepper to taste

Directions:

1. Heat up the butter in a pan that fits your air fryer over medium heat.
2. Add the onions, garlic, dried and fresh rosemary, stock, soy sauce, salt and pepper; stir and simmer for 2-3 minutes
3. Add the cornstarch mixture, whisk, cook for 2 minutes more and take off the heat
4. Add the chicken, toss gently and place the pan in the fryer; cook at 370 °F for 20 minutes. Divide between plates and serve hot.

Chicken Pasta Salad

Cooking Time: 27 minutes

Servings: 2

Ingredients:

- 3 chicken breasts
- 1 medium bag frozen vegetables of choice
- 1 cup rigatoni or pasta of choice; cooked
- Paprika
- Garlic and herb seasoning
- Italian dressing
- Black pepper
- Ground parsley
- Oil spray

Directions:

1. Wash the chicken breasts and season with paprika, garlic and herb seasoning and a tbsp. of the Italian dressing. Top a little with black pepper and ground parsley. Mist the air fryer

with oil, then add the marinated chicken breasts. Spray oil over the chicken as well. Cook at 360 °F for 15 minutes

2. Halfway through, flip the chicken breasts and season with pepper and parsley. Spray over with oil and allow to cook all the way

3. While the chicken is cooking, empty a bag of frozen vegetables into a bowl and season with the garlic and herb dressing and some Italian dressing. Mix well. Spray another air fryer and add in the vegetables. Cook for 12 minutes at 380°F.

4. Dice the cooked chicken while waiting for the vegetables to cook. Season the cooked with some garlic and herb seasoning, along with some parsley and Italian dressing

5. Mix well, tasting to your preference. Add the diced chicken to the mix, mixing well. Once the vegetables have finished cooking, add to the chicken and pasta mixture and incorporate thoroughly. Serve

Flourless Chicken Cordon Bleu

Cooking Time: 8 minutes

Servings: 2

Ingredients:

- 2 chicken breasts
- 1 slice ham
- 1 slice cheddar cheese
- 1 small egg; beaten
- 1 tbsp. thyme
- 1 tbsp. oats
- 1 tbsp. tarragon
- 1 tbsp. soft cheese
- 1 tsp. garlic purée
- 1 tsp. parsley
- Salt and pepper; to taste

Directions:

1. Preheat air fryer to 356 °F. On a chopping board, chop the chicken breasts at a side angle to right near the corner. Sprinkle the chicken on

all sides with salt, pepper and tarragon

2. In a mixing bowl, mix the soft cheese, garlic and parsley well. Place a layer of the cheese mixture in the middle of the breast along with ½ slice each of the cheddar cheese and ham. Once done, press the chicken down to seal

3. Place the egg and oats in different bowls. Add the thyme to the oats bowl and mix well. Roll the chicken in the oats first, then in the egg, then back to the oats

4. Place chicken pieces on a baking sheet in your air fryer and cook for 30 minutes at 356 °F. After 20 minutes, turn it over so both sides cook evenly. Serve.

Pork and Sprouts

Preparation Time: 35 minutes

Servings: 4

Ingredients:

- 1½ lbs. Brussels sprouts; trimmed
- 1 lb. pork tenderloin; cubed
- 1 garlic clove; minced
- 1/2 cup sour cream

- 2 tbsp. rosemary; chopped.
- 2 tbsp. olive oil
- Salt and black pepper to taste

Directions:

1. In a pan that fits your air fryer, mix the pork with the oil, rosemary, salt, pepper, garlic, salt and pepper; toss well.
2. Place the pan in the fryer and cook at 400 °F for 17 minutes
3. Next add the sprouts and the sour cream and toss
4. Place the pan in the fryer and cook for 8 more minutes. Divide everything into bowls and serve.

Beef, Arugula and Leeks

Preparation Time: 22 minutes

Servings: 4

Ingredients:

- 1 lb. ground beef
- 2 tbsp. tomato paste
- 5 oz. baby arugula
- 1 tbsp. olive oil
- 3 leeks; roughly chopped.
- Salt and black pepper to taste

Directions:

1. In a pan that fits your air fryer, mix the beef with the leeks, salt, pepper, oil and the tomato paste; toss well
2. Place the pan in the fryer and cook at 380 °F for 12 minutes
3. Add the arugula and toss. Divide into bowls and serve.

BBQ Pork Ribs

Servings: 4

Preparation Time: 15 minutes

Cooking Time: 26 minutes

Ingredients

- 1¾ pounds pork ribs
- ¼ cup honey, divided
- ¾ cup BBQ sauce
- 2 tablespoons tomato ketchup
- 1 tablespoon Worcestershire sauce*
- ½ teaspoon garlic powder
- 1 tablespoon soy sauce
- Freshly ground white pepper, to taste

Directions:

1. In a bowl, mix together 3 tablespoons of honey and the remaining ingredients except pork ribs.
2. Add the pork ribs and generously coat with the mixture.

3. Refrigerate to marinate for about 20 minutes.
4. Set the temperature of air fryer to 355 degrees F. Grease an air fryer basket
5. Arrange ribs into the prepared air fryer basket in a single layer.
6. Air fry for about 13 minutes per side.
7. Remove from air fryer and transfer the ribs onto plates.
8. Drizzle with the remaining honey and serve immediately.

Nutrition:

Calories: 691, Carbohydrate: 37.7g, Protein: 53.1g, Fat: 31.3g, Sugar: 32.2g, Sodium: 991mg

(Note - Worcestershire sauce* - The other ingredients that make up this savory sauce usually include onions, molasses, high fructose corn syrup: depending on the country of production), salt, garlic, tamarind, cloves, chili pepper extract, water and natural flavorings.

Bacon Wrapped Pork tenderloin

Servings: 4

Preparation Time: 15 minutes

Cooking Time: 30 minutes

Ingredients

- 4 bacon strips
- 1: 1½ pound pork tenderloins
- 2 tablespoons Dijon mustard

Directions:

1. Coat the tenderloin evenly with mustard.
2. Wrap the tenderloin with bacon strips.
3. Set the temperature of air fryer to 360 degrees F. Grease an air fryer basket.
4. Arrange pork tenderloin into the prepared air fryer basket.
5. Air fry for about 15 minutes.
6. Flip and air fry for another 10-15 minutes.

7. Remove from air fryer and transfer the pork tenderloin onto a platter, wait for about 5 minutes before slicing.
8. Cut the tenderloin into desired size slices and serve.

Nutrition:

Calories: 504, Carbohydrate: 0.8g, Protein:61.9, Fat: 26.2g, Sugar: 9.1g, Sodium: 867mg

Nut Crusted Rack of Lamb

Servings: 5

Preparation Time: 15 minutes

Cooking Time: 35 minutes

Ingredients

- 1 egg
- 1 tablespoon olive oil
- 1 garlic clove, minced
- 1¾ pounds rack of lamb
- 1 tablespoon breadcrumbs
- 3 ounces almonds, finely chopped
- Salt and ground black pepper, as required

Directions:

1. In a bowl, mix together the oil, garlic, salt, and black pepper.
2. Coat the rack of lamb evenly with oil mixture.
3. Crack the egg in a shallow bowl and beat well.
4. In another bowl, mix together the breadcrumbs and almonds.

5. Dip the rack of lamb in beaten egg and then, coat with almond mixture.
6. Set the temperature of air fryer to 220 degrees F. Grease an air fryer basket.
7. Place the rack of lamb into the prepared air fryer basket.
8. Air fry for about 30 minutes and then 5 more minutes at 390 degrees F.
9. Remove from air fryer and place the rack of lamb onto a cutting board for about 5 minutes
10. With a sharp knife, cut the rack of lamb into individual chops and serve.

Nutrition:

Calories: 340, Carbohydrate: 4.1g, Protein: 31g, Fat: 21.9g, Sugar: 0.7g, Sodium: 140mg

Crispy Potatoes and Parsley

Preparation Time: 10 minutes

Cooking time: 10 minutes

Servings: 4

Ingredients:

- 1 pound gold potatoes, cut into wedges
- 2 tablespoons olive

- ¼ cup parsley leaves, chopped
- Juice from ½ lemon
- Salt and black pepper to the taste

Directions:

1. Rub potatoes with salt, pepper, lemon juice and olive oil, put them in your air fryer and cook at 350 °F for 10 minutes.
2. Divide among plates, sprinkle parsley on top and serve.

Nutrition:

Calories: 163; Fat: 5g; Fiber: 2g; Carbs: 4g; Protein: 8g

Sweet and Spicy Parsnips

Preparation Time: 15 minutes

Cooking Time: 44 minutes

Servings: 6

Ingredients:

- 2 pounds parsnip, peeled and cut into 1-inch chunks
- 2 tablespoons honey
- 1 tablespoon butter, melted
- 1 tablespoon dried parsley flakes, crushed
- ¼ teaspoon red pepper flakes, crushed
- Salt and ground black pepper, to taste

Directions:

1. Preheat the Air fryer to 355 degrees F and grease an Air fryer basket.
2. Mix the parsnips and butter in a bowl and toss to coat well.
3. Arrange the parsnip chunks in the Air fryer basket and cook for about 40 minutes.

4. Mix the remaining ingredients in another large bowl and stir in the parsnip chunks.
5. Transfer the parsnip chunks in the Air fryer basket and cook for about 4 minutes.
6. Dish out the parsnip chunks onto serving plates and serve hot.

Nutrition:

Calories: 155, Fat: 2.4g, Carbohydrates: 33.1g, Sugar: 13g, Protein: 1.9g, Sodium: 57mg

Sautéed Spinach

Preparation Time: 24 minutes

Servings: 2

Ingredients:

- 1 small onion; chopped
- 1 garlic clove, minced
- 6-oz fresh spinach

- 2 tbsp. olive oil
- Salt and ground black pepper; as your liking

Directions:

1. Set the temperature of air fryer to 340 °F. In an air fryer pan, heat the oil for about 2 minutes.
2. Add the onion and garlic and air fry for about 3 minutes.
3. Add the spinach, salt and black pepper and air fry for about 4 more minutes.
4. Remove from air fryer and transfer the spinach mixture onto serving plates. Serve hot.

Kale and Olives

Preparation Time: 20 minutes

Servings: 4

Ingredients

- 1 an ½ lb. kale, torn
- 2 tbsp. olive oil
- 1 tbsp. hot paprika
- 2 tbsp. black olives, pitted and sliced
- Salt and black pepper to taste.

Directions:

1. In a pan that fits the air fryer, combine all the Ingredients: and toss.
2. Put the pan in your air fryer, cook at 370 °F for 15 minutes, divide between plates and serve

Nutrition:

Calories: 154; Fat: 3g; Fiber: 2g; Carbs: 4g; Protein: 6g

Sweet & Spicy Parsnips

Servings: 6

Preparation Time: 15 minutes

Cooking Time: 44 minutes

Ingredients

- 2 pounds parsnip, peeled and cut into 1-inch chunks
- 2 tablespoons honey
- 1 tablespoon butter, melted
- 1 tablespoon dried parsley flakes, crushed
- ¼ teaspoon red pepper flakes, crushed
- Salt and ground black pepper, as required

Directions:

1. Set the temperature of air fryer to 355 degrees F. Grease an air fryer basket.
2. In a large bowl, mix together the parsnips and butter.

3. Arrange parsnip chunks into the prepared air fryer basket in a single layer.
4. Air fry for about 40 minutes.
5. Meanwhile, in another large bowl, mix well the remaining ingredients.
6. After 40 minutes, transfer parsnips into the bowl of honey mixture and toss to coat well.
7. Again, arrange the parsnip chunks into air fryer basket in a single layer.
8. Air fry for 3-4 more minutes.
9. Remove from air fryer and transfer the parsnip chunks onto serving plates.
10. Serve hot.

Nutrition:

Calories: 155, Carbohydrate: 33.1g, Protein: 1.9g, Fat: 2.4g, Sugar: 13g, Sodium: 57mg

Air fryer Golden Lentil and Spinach Soup

Preparation Time: 10 minutes

Cooking Time: 25 minutes

Servings: 4

Ingredients:

- 2 teaspoons of olive oil
- ½ yellow onion, diced
- 1 celery stock, diced
- 2 carrots, peeled and diced
- 4 garlic cloves, minced
- 2 teaspoons ground cumin
- 1 teaspoon ground turmeric
- 1 teaspoon kosher salt
- 1 teaspoon dried thyme
- ¼ teaspoon freshly ground black pepper
- 1 cup dry brown lentils, rinsed well
- 4 cups low-sodium vegetable broth
- 8 ounces baby spinach

Directions:

1. Choose saute function of the air fryer and add oil. When hot, add onions, carrots, and celery. Saute, occasionally stirring, until tender, about 5 minutes.
2. Add garlic, cumin, turmeric, thyme, salt, and pepper. Cook and stir for one minute.
3. Stir in lentil and broth.
4. Place lid on air fryer and put the valve to "sealing." Press manual high pressure and set a timer for 12 minutes.
5. After 12 minutes, quick release pressure and then carefully remove the lid when done. Stir in the spinach, and add salt and pepper to taste.

Nutrition:

Calories – 134 Protein – 9 g. Fat – 3 g. Carbs – 17 g.

Japanese Udon Noodle Soup

Preparation Time: 10 minutes

Cooking Time: 27 minutes

Servings: 2

Ingredients:

- 3 oz. Japanese udon noodles, cooked and drained
- ½ cup mushrooms
- ½ cup baby carrots
- ½ cup green bell peppers
- ½ cup celery
- ½ cup bamboo shoots
- 2 garlic cloves, minced
- ½ green chilli, finely chopped
- 1 teaspoon rice vinegar soy sauce
- ½ inch ginger, minced
- 1 green onion white
- 1 teaspoon rice wine vinegar
- 1 teaspoon red chilli sauce
- 1 tablespoon sesame oil

- Bean sprouts and green onions, for garnish
- Salt and pepper, to taste

Directions:

1. Put the oil, ginger, garlic, baby carrots and onions in the Air fryer and select "Sauté".
2. Sauté for 4 minutes and add bamboo shoots, celery, green bell peppers, mushrooms, soy sauce, rice wine vinegar, chilli sauce.
3. Set the Air fryer to "Soup" and cook for 13 minutes at high pressure.
4. Release the pressure naturally and add cooked udon noodles.
5. Season with salt and black pepper and garnish with onion greens and bean sprouts.

Nutrition:

Calories: 179; Total Fat: 3.9g; Carbs: 30g; Sugars: 2.7g; Protein: 3.6g

Air fryer Italian Beef Stew

Preparation Time: 10 minutes

Cooking Time: 35 minutes

Servings: 6

Ingredients:

- 3 pounds of beef stew
- 4 carrots, diced
- 1 onion, diced
- 8-ounce baby portabella mushrooms, sliced
- 15 ounce diced tomatoes, canned
- 24-ounces of beef broth
- 3 tablespoons of white flour
- 1 teaspoon of dried basil leaves
- 1 teaspoon of dried thyme leaves
- 1 teaspoon of salt
- 1 teaspoon of pepper
- dried parsley

Directions:

1. Place meat in the air fryer.
2. Add in carrots, broth, flour, basil, thyme, salt, pepper, and tomatoes to air fryer and stir.
3. Close the lid.
4. Cook on high pressure for 35 minutes.
5. Quick release the pressure and carefully remove the lid.
6. Stir in the mushroom, stir the soup and then serve.

Nutrition:

Calories – 385 Protein – 54 g. Fat – 12 g. Carbs – 12 g.

Crispy Kale Chips (Vegan)

Servings: 3

Cooking Time: 7 minutes

Ingredients:

- 3 cups kale leaves, stems removed
- 1 tablespoon olive oil
- Salt and pepper, to taste

Directions

1. In a bowl, combine all of the ingredients. Toss to coat the kale leaves with oil, salt, and pepper.
2. Arrange the kale leaves on the double layer rack and insert inside the air fryer.
3. Close the air fryer and cook for 7 minutes at 370 degrees F.
4. Allow to cool before serving.

Nutrition

Calories: 48; Carbs: 1.4g; Protein: 0.7g; Fat: 4.8g

Spicy Chicken with Lemon and Parsley in A Packet

Servings: 4

Cooking Time: 45 minutes

Ingredients:

- 2 pounds chicken thighs
- ¼ cup smoked paprika
- ½ teaspoon liquid smoke seasoning
- 1 ½ tablespoon cayenne pepper
- 4 lemons, halved
- ½ cup parsley leaves
- Salt and pepper to taste

Directions

1. Preheat the air fryer at 375 degrees F.
2. Place the grill pan accessory in the air fryer.
3. In a large piece of foil, place the chicken and season with paprika, liquid smoke seasoning, salt, pepper, and cayenne pepper.
4. Top with lemon and parsley.
5. Place on the grill and cook for 45 minutes.

Nutrition

Calories: 546; Carbs: 10.4g; Protein: 39.2g; Fat: 39.1g

Fennel Spread

Preparation Time: 25 minutes

Servings: 8

Ingredients:

- 3 fennel bulbs; trimmed and cut into wedges
- 4 garlic cloves; minced
- 3 tbsp. olive oil
- ¼ cup parmesan; grated

- A pinch of salt and black pepper

Directions:

1. Put the fennel in the air fryer's basket and bake at 380 °F for 20 minutes.
2. In a blender, combine the roasted fennel with the rest of the ingredients and pulse well
3. Put the spread in a ramekin, introduce it in the fryer and cook at 380 °F for 5 minutes more
4. Divide into bowls and serve as a dip.

Nutrition:

Calories: 240; Fat: 11g; Fiber: 3g; Carbs: 4g; Protein: 12g

Beans and Veggie Burgers

Preparation Time: 20 minutes

Cooking Time: 23 minutes

Servings: 4

Ingredients:

- 1 cup cooked black beans
- 2 cups boiled potatoes, peeled and mashed
- 1 cup fresh mushrooms, chopped
- 1 cup fresh spinach, chopped
- 6 cups fresh baby greens
- 2 teaspoons Chile lime seasoning
- Olive oil cooking spray

Directions:

1. Preheat the Air fryer to 375 degrees F and grease an Air fryer basket.
2. Mix together potatoes, spinach, beans, mushrooms and Chile lime seasoning in a large bowl.

3. Make 4 equal-sized patties from this mixture and place the patties into the prepared Air fryer basket.
4. Spray with olive oil cooking spray and cook for about 20 minutes, flipping once in between.
5. Set the Air fryer to 90 degrees F and cook for about 3 more minutes.
6. Dish out in a platter and serve alongside the baby greens.

Nutrition:

Calories: 249, Fat: 1.1g, Carbohydrates: 48.8g, Sugar: 2.9g, Protein: 13.7g, Sodium: 47mg

Apple Hand Pies

Preparation Time: 5 minutes

Cooking Time: 8 minutes

Servings: 6

Ingredients:

- 15-ounces no-sugar-added apple pie filling
- 1 store-bought crust

Directions:

1. Lay out pie crust and slice into equal-sized squares.
2. Place 2 tbsp. filling into each square and seal crust with a fork.
3. Pour into the Oven rack/basket. Place the Rack on the middle-shelf of the Air fryer oven. Set temperature to 390 °F, and set time to 8 minutes until golden in color.

Nutrition:

Calories – 278, Protein – 5 g., Fat – 10 g.,Carbs – 17 g.

Brownie Muffins

Preparation Time: 10 minutes

Cooking Time: 10 minutes

Servings: 12

Ingredients:

- 1 egg
- 1 package Betty Crocker fudge brownie mix
- ¼ cup walnuts, chopped
- 1/3 cup vegetable oil
- 2 teaspoons water

Directions:

1. Grease 12 muffin molds. Set aside.
2. In a bowl, put all ingredients together.
3. Place the mixture into the prepared muffin molds.
4. Press "Power Button" of Air Fry Oven and turn the dial to select the "Air Fry" mode.
5. Press the Time button and again turn the dial to set the cooking time to 10 minutes.

6. Now push the Temp button and rotate the dial to set the temperature at 300 degrees F.
7. Press "Start/Pause" button to start.
8. When the unit beeps to show that it is preheated, open the lid.
9. Arrange the muffin molds in "Air Fry Basket" and insert in the oven.
10. Place the muffin molds onto a wire rack to cool for about 10 minutes.
11. Carefully, invert the muffins onto the wire rack to completely cool before serving.

Nutrition:

Calories – 168, Protein – 2 g., Fat – 8.9 g., Carbs – 20.8 g.

Doughnuts Pudding

Preparation Time: 15 minutes

Cooking Time: 1 hour; Serves 4

Ingredients:

- 6 glazed doughnuts, cut into small pieces
- ¾ cup frozen sweet cherries
- ½ cup raisins
- 4 egg yolks
- ½ cup semi-sweet chocolate baking chips
- 1 teaspoon ground cinnamon
- ¼ cup sugar
- 1½ cups whipping cream

Directions:

1. Preheat the Air fryer to 310 degrees F and grease a baking dish lightly.
2. Mix doughnut pieces, cherries, raisins, chocolate chips, sugar, and cinnamon in a large bowl.
3. Whisk the egg yolks with whipping cream in another bowl until well combined.

4. Combine the egg yolk mixture into the doughnut mixture and mix well.
5. Arrange the doughnuts mixture evenly into the baking dish and transfer into the Air fryer basket.
6. Cook for about 60 minutes and dish out to serve warm.

Nutrition:

Calories: 786, Fat: 43.2g, Carbohydrates: 9.3g, Sugar: 60.7g, Protein: 11g, Sodium: 419mg

Chocolate Banana Pastries

Preparation Time: 27 minutes

Servings: 4

Ingredients:

- 2 bananas; peeled and sliced
- 1 puff pastry sheet
- 1/2 cup Nutella

Directions:

1. Cut the pastry sheet into 4 equal-sized squares. Spread Nutella evenly on each square of pastry. Divide the banana slices over Nutella. Fold each square into a triangle and with wet fingers, slightly press the edges. Then with a fork, press the edges firmly
2. Set the temperature of air fryer to 375 °F. Lightly, grease an air fryer basket. Arrange pastries into the prepared air fryer basket in a single layer. Air fry for about 10 to 12 minutes. Remove from air fryer and transfer the pastries onto a platter. Serve warm

Apple Tart

Servings: 3

Preparation Time: 10 minutes

Cooking Time: 25 minutes

Ingredients

- 1 egg yolk
- 2½ ounces butter, chopped and divided
- 3½ ounces flour
- 1 ounce sugar
- 1 large granny smith apple, peeled, cored and cut into 12 wedges

Directions:

1. In a bowl, add half of the butter, flour, and egg yolk and mix until a soft dough forms.
2. Now, put the dough onto a floured surface and roll into a 6-inch round circle.
3. Set the temperature of air fryer to 390 degrees F.

4. In a baking pan, add the remaining butter and sprinkle with sugar.
5. Top with the apple wedges in a circular pattern.
6. Place the rolled dough over apple wedges and gently press along the edges of the pan.
7. Arrange the pan into an air fryer basket.
8. Air fry for about 25 minutes.
9. Remove from the air fryer and serve warm.

Nutrition:

Calories: 382, Carbohydrate: 45.2g, Protein: 4.7g, Fat: 21.1g, Sugar: 17.3g, Sodium: 140mg

Crispy Banana Split

Servings: 8

Preparation Time: 15 minutes

Cooking Time: 14 minutes

Ingredients

- 2 eggs
- 3 tablespoons coconut oil
- 1 cup panko breadcrumbs
- ½ cup corn flour
- 4 bananas, peeled and halved lengthwise
- 3 tablespoons sugar
- ¼ teaspoon ground cinnamon
- 2 tablespoons walnuts, chopped

Directions:

1. In a medium skillet, heat the oil over medium heat and cook breadcrumbs for about 3-4 minutes or until golden browned and crumbled, stirring continuously.
2. Transfer the breadcrumbs into a shallow bowl and set aside to cool.

3. In a second bowl, place the corn flour.
4. In a third bowl, whisk the eggs.
5. Coat the banana slices with flour and then, dip into eggs and finally, coat evenly with the breadcrumbs.
6. In a small bowl, mix together the sugar and cinnamon
7. Set the temperature of air fryer to 280 degrees F. Grease an air fryer basket.
8. Arrange banana slices into the prepared air fryer basket in a single layer and sprinkle with cinnamon sugar
9. Air fry for about 10 minutes.
10. Remove from air fryer and transfer the banana slices onto plates to cool slightly
11. Sprinkle with chopped walnuts and serve.

Nutrition:

Calories: 216, Carbohydrate: 26g, Protein: 3.4g, Fat: 8.8g, Sugar: 11.9g, Sodium: 16mg

Delicious Grilled Pineapple

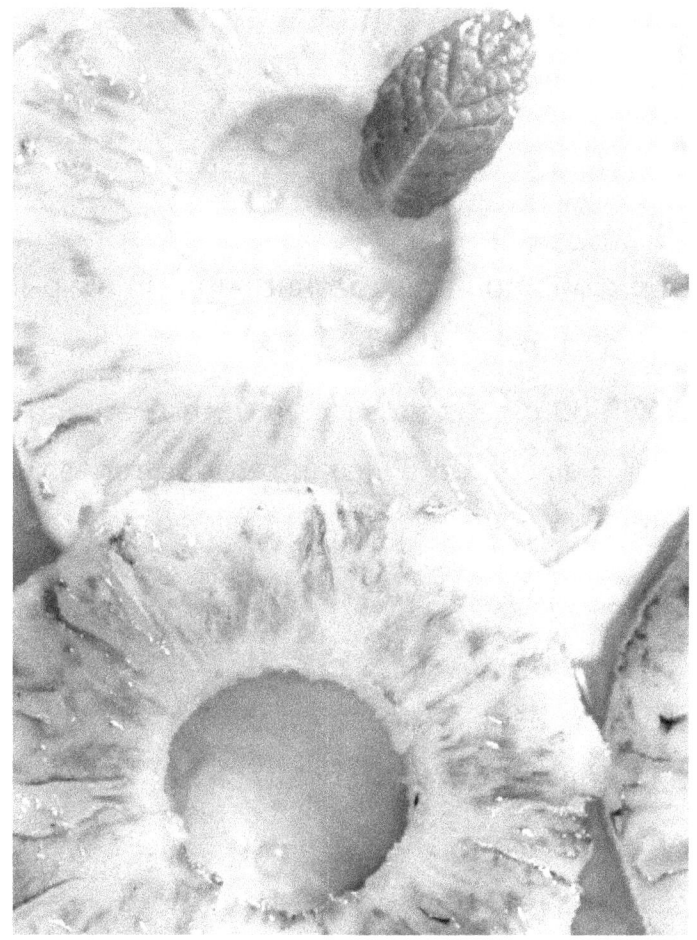

Servings: 4

Preparation Time: 5 minutes

Cooking Time: 20 minutes

Ingredients

- 4 pineapple slices
- 1 tsp ground cinnamon
- 4 tbsp coconut sugar

Directions

1. Add cinnamon and coconut sugar in a zip-lock bag and mix well.
2. Now add pineapple slices into the bag and shake until well coated. Place in refrigerator for half an hour.
3. Preheat the air fryer at 180 C/ 356 F for 5 minutes.
4. Place pineapple slices on the air fryer's wire rack and grill them for 10 minutes.
5. After 10 minutes flip pineapple slices to other side and grill them for 10 minutes more.
6. Serve and enjoy.

Nutrition Values:

Calories 141; Fat 0 g; Carbohydrates 29.5 g; Sugar 10 g; Protein 1 g; Cholesterol 0 mg

Lemon Blueberry Muffin

Servings: 12

Preparation Time: 10 minutes

Cooking Time: 10 minutes

Ingredients

- 2 eggs
- 1 tsp vanilla
- 2 1/2 cups almond flour

- 1 tbsp lemon juice
- 1 cup blueberries
- 1/4 cup olive oil
- 1/2 cup coconut cream
- 1/2 cup monk fruit

Directions

1. In a small bowl, mix together almond flour and monk fruit and set aside.
2. In a mixing bowl, combine together coconut cream, eggs, vanilla, and lemon juice.
3. Add almond flour mixture to the coconut cream mixture and stir until well blended.
4. Pour the batter into silicone cupcake holders.
5. Place in air fryer and cook for 10 minutes at 320 F/ 160 C.
6. Serve and enjoy.

Nutrition Values

Calories 211; Fat 19 g; Carbohydrates 7.4 g; Sugar 2.5 g; Protein 6.3 g; Cholesterol 27 mg

Pecan Brownies

Preparation Time: 30 minutes

Servings: 6

Ingredients:

- 1 large egg.
- ¼ cup chopped pecans
- ¼ cup low-carb, sugar-free chocolate chips.
- ¼ cup unsalted butter; softened.
- ½ cup blanched finely ground almond flour.
- ½ cup powdered erythritol
- 2 tbsp. unsweetened cocoa powder
- ½ tsp. baking powder.

Directions:

1. Take a large bowl, mix almond flour, erythritol, cocoa powder and baking powder. Stir in butter and egg.
2. Fold in pecans and chocolate chips. Scoop mixture into 6-inch round baking pan. Place pan into the air fryer basket.

3. Adjust the temperature to 300 Degrees F and set the timer for 20 minutes. When fully cooked a toothpick inserted in center will come out clean. Allow 20 minutes to fully cool and firm up.

Nutrition:

Calories: 215; Protein: 4.2g; Fiber: 2.8g; Fat: 18.9g; Carbs: 21.8g

Notes

www.ingramcontent.com/pod-product-compliance
Lightning Source LLC
Chambersburg PA
CBHW070933080526
44589CB00013B/1500